REAL BUGS

PREDATORS

IN 3-D

Advance PUBLISHERS

DeAGOSTINI COLLECT & DISCOVER

ROBBER FLY

Once it has spotted its target, the robber fly swoops down on its victim, moving in for the kill.

With its huge appetite, the robber fly isn't choosy about what it eats. It even attacks insects that are bigger than it, such grasshoppers and dragonflies. Some types of robber fly will even steal baby bees from a nest. This is how this fly got its name.

SURPRISE ATTACK

The robber fly hunts by day. It seizes its prey in midflight and quickly stabs it with its proboscis, which is sharp enough to pierce the toughest skin. Then it carries its victim off to a quiet spot, where the robber fly sucks out the victim's insides, leaving only the hard outer covering. Sometimes the robber fly is lazy and sits on a log or the ground waiting for unsuspecting prey to wander by. Thick bristles around its bulging eyes protect them from struggling victims.

PLAYING SAFE

Robber flies are so fierce that they may even eat each other! The only time it is safe for the male fly to mate with the female is when she is busy eating. Otherwise, she may turn on him.

SIZING UP

BEASTLY FACTS

- **SCIENTIFIC NAME:** *Asilus crabroniformis*
- **SIZE:** 0.78–1.6 inch long
- **LIVES:** Europe, Asia, and North Africa
- **EATS:** Adult eats insects; larva eats dead bugs

1.6 inch

EMPEROR SCORPION

The biggest scorpion in the world is the emperor scorpion. It has massive razor-sharp pincers and prowls the forest at night in search of food.

From the tip of its head to the end of its tail, the emperor scorpion is over 5.9 inches (15cm) long. This huge scorpion eats anything from bugs to small lizards and mammals. Yet despite its fearsome appearance, large stinger, and massive pincers, the emperor scorpion is not dangerous to humans.

OUT AT NIGHT

The emperor scorpion lives in the hot and humid forests of central Africa. It is found among the fallen leaves that collect at the base of trees. Like most scorpions, it is nocturnal, coming out only at night. The emperor scorpion can live for a surprisingly long time—over eight years.

BIG AND STRONG

Because of its size, this scorpion does not need powerful venom to kill. It holds its prey with its scissorlike pincers and stings it several times until it stops struggling. The scorpion takes the food back to its burrow, where it pulls its prey apart. The prey is shredded further by a smaller set of pincers, which the scorpion uses to place the food in its mouth.

EMPEROR SCORPION

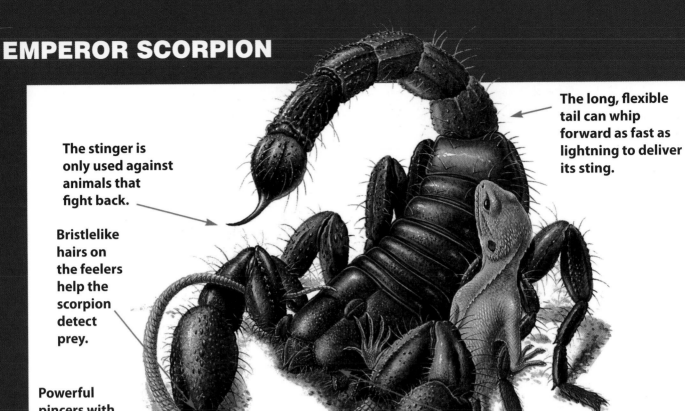

The stinger is only used against animals that fight back.

Bristlelike hairs on the feelers help the scorpion detect prey.

Powerful pincers with razor-sharp edges can rip even large prey to bits.

The long, flexible tail can whip forward as fast as lightning to deliver its sting.

The mouthparts have tiny pincers that cut food into chunks small enough to swallow.

Small Talk

GREEN AND GLOWING
Because emperor scorpions are black and come out only at night, they are very difficult to see. Scientists who study these scorpions in the wild take lamps that give off a special kind of light called ultraviolet light. The scorpion's outer shell glows bright green when it is lit up with ultraviolet light.

DANGER SIGNS
Scorpions with big pincers—like the emperor scorpion—do not usually need strong venom because they are strong enough to hold their prey still. A scorpion is more likely to be dangerous if its pincers are small. Small pincers mean the scorpion needs to rely on venom to overpower its prey.

CAUTIOUS MOVER
When he wants to mate, the male emperor scorpion approaches the female slowly and very carefully. Once he is quite sure she knows he is there and that she no longer thinks he might be a tasty snack, he moves forward.

MATING DANCE
The two of them then lock their pincers together and pull each other around. It looks as though they are doing some sort of strange, complicated dance. In fact, the male is trying to position the female for mating. This mating "dance" can last from several hours to two days. A few months after the scorpions have mated, the female gives birth. She usually has between 20 and 50 babies.

HITCHING A LIFT

Baby scorpions are small white creatures that look a bit like wood lice, or pill bugs. As each baby is born, the mother helps it crawl onto her back. While the babies are there, they rely on her completely for transportation, food, and safety. After a few weeks, the babies shed their skins. They then look like miniature versions of the mother. The babies stay with the mother for several weeks. When the young scorpions are able to feed themselves, they wander off.

A CHANGE OF CLOTHES

Like all bugs that have a hard skeleton on the outside, the emperor scorpion has to shed its skin in order to grow. It usually does this once a year throughout its life.

BEASTLY FACTS

- **SCIENTIFIC NAME:** *Pandinus imperator*
- **SIZE:** 5.9 inches
- **LIVES:** Rain forests of central Africa
- **EATS:** Bugs, lizards, small mammals

SIZING UP

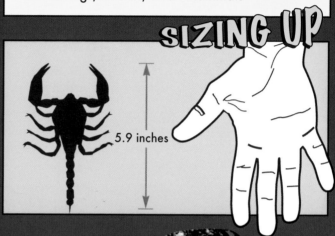

5.9 inches

Is it true...

that when scorpions fight they can sting each other to death?

No. Scorpions cannot be hurt by their own venom, so they cannot sting each other—or themselves—to death. Their powerful pincers, however, are quite capable of ripping their opponent to pieces.

The babies on the mother's back are soft and helpless

3-D

MINIBEASTS

JUMPING SPIDER
Among the leaves on the forest floor, a male jumping spider stalks its prey. With its six small eyes watching out for danger, its two larger front eyes scan the ground ahead for food. Suddenly, it spots a small beetle nearly 11.8 inches (30cm) away. The spider tenses and then springs through the air, landing on top of its victim. Its fangs sink into the writhing beetle's back and inject it with a fast-acting poison.

The crafty trapdoor spider uses its burrow to capture bugs. But when an enemy drops by, the spider vanishes as if by magic.

Trapdoor spiders are underground architects, building cleverly designed burrows. They use them as nests, hiding places when hunting insects, and protection from their enemies. Hundreds of different types of trapdoor spiders live all over the world.

BUILDING A HOME

Trapdoor spiders make deep burrows. Using their very sharp fangs like rakes, they dig the soil. They sweep it into little lumps, and then brush it outside. Once the burrow is finished, they close the top with a hinged lid, or trapdoor, which is level with the ground,

HOUSE PROUD

Some burrow lids are thin flaps, but most are thick slabs built up from layers of silk and soil. The spider spends a lot of time carefully making sure the lid is a perfect fit.

KSTERS

THE WAITING GAME

1 The spider sits under the trapdoor with its front legs sticking out from under the lid, . . . waiting

2 The hairs on the spider's legs pick up vibrations on the ground. It knows an insect is approaching and pounces.

3 It takes some spiders just 0.03 seconds to grab their victim. That's faster than the time it takes to blink! They then inject their victim with poison and pull it down the burrow to be eaten.

OPEN AND SHUT CASE

The lid has a silk hinge so that it can be opened and closed, like a trapdoor. This is how the spider got its name. When it is finally satisfied with the lid, the spider pulls some moss and plants over the lid so that it is hidden. Now the spider sets its trap.

HUNTING FOR FOOD

Trapdoor spiders hunt from home. Most live in damp places, where there are plenty of insects. This means they don't have to wait long before an unsuspecting victim comes along.

WATCHING AND WAITING

The spider sits at the top of the burrow with the lid slightly open. Its front legs stick out under the lid. Then it waits to pounce, like the spider in the pictures above.

TRIP WIRES

Some spiders lay complicated traps using twigs or silken wires. The spider arranges these in lines coming out from the burrow entrance like the spokes of a wheel. If a wire or twig moves, the spider knows that a small animal has stumbled across it and rushes out to the attack.

TRAPDOOR TRICKSTERS

WATCH OUT

The trapdoor spider stays in the same spot for most of its life, so its enemies often go hunting for it. Its worst enemy is the spider-hunting wasp, which forces its way into the spider's burrow, paralyses it with its sting, and lays an egg. When the wasp grub hatches, it eats the spider while it's still alive.

CLINGING ON FOR LIFE

Trapdoor spiders have different ways of outwitting their enemies. When an enemy attempts to force open the lid to the burrow, some spiders cling to the bottom of the lid, trying to resist the intruder. The California trapdoor spider can hold down a force 38 times heavier than itself. That's like one adult man having a tug-of-war contest with three and a half football teams on the other side—and winning!

BOTTOMS UP

The back of the flat-bottomed trapdoor spider looks as if it has been cut off. Its end is covered with a special kind of armor plating. The bottom of the burrow fits this spider's body exactly. A threatened flat-bottomed trapdoor spider can scoot down the burrow and plug it with its body, like a cork in a bottle (right). All the predator finds is the spider's hard, flat body, which it can't grip properly. The spider is safe.

This trapdoor spider heads for home. Its best defense is its craftily designed burrow.

Bottoms up! The spider blocks its burrow. The predator can't grip the spider's bottom, which is covered in a kind of armor plating, keeping it safe.

FRONT DOOR, BACK DOOR

Some spiders build burrows with side chambers and more than one entrance. These act as escape routes. When a predator appears at one opening, the spider darts up the other and escapes (below).

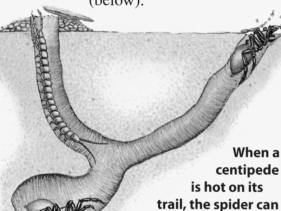

When a centipede is hot on its trail, the spider can scurry out of his own back door to safety.

IN HIDING

Other trapdoor spiders line the lower part of their burrows with silk. They leave an open collar, like the top of a bag, halfway up. The spider makes a pear-shaped pellet from silk, saliva, and mud. This sits in a hollowed-out chamber at the side of the collar (right). If a hungry centipede, or other predator, peers down the burrow, the spider tugs at the collar. The pellet topples over, making a barrier to hide behind, and the spider has vanished!

FLOOD WARNING

It's not just hungry predators that trapdoor spiders have to cope with. Sometimes water floods their burrows. To avoid drowning, some spiders build a side chamber halfway up the burrow. They can sit here safe and dry as the water at the bottom rises (right).

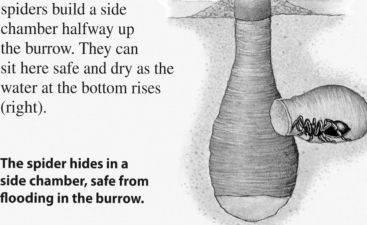

The spider hides in a side chamber, safe from flooding in the burrow.

Small Talk

- Trapdoor spiders will pounce on anything that moves near their burrows. Sometimes they accidentally catch something that doesn't taste good. If this happens, the spider flings the offending animal out from its burrow.
- A female trapdoor spider may spend her whole life inside her burrow. As she gets bigger, she makes her burrow bigger too

Chased by a bull ant, the spider scrambles into its home and hides behind its lid of silk and mud.

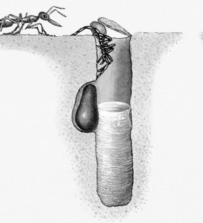

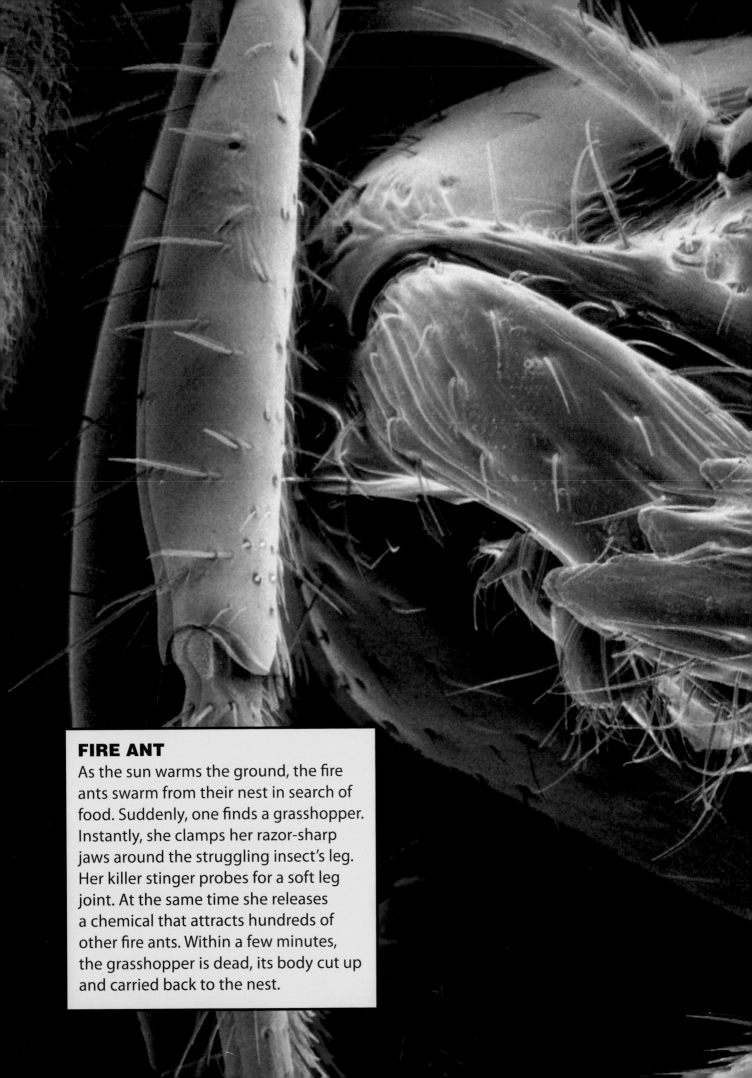

FIRE ANT

As the sun warms the ground, the fire ants swarm from their nest in search of food. Suddenly, one finds a grasshopper. Instantly, she clamps her razor-sharp jaws around the struggling insect's leg. Her killer stinger probes for a soft leg joint. At the same time she releases a chemical that attracts hundreds of other fire ants. Within a few minutes, the grasshopper is dead, its body cut up and carried back to the nest.

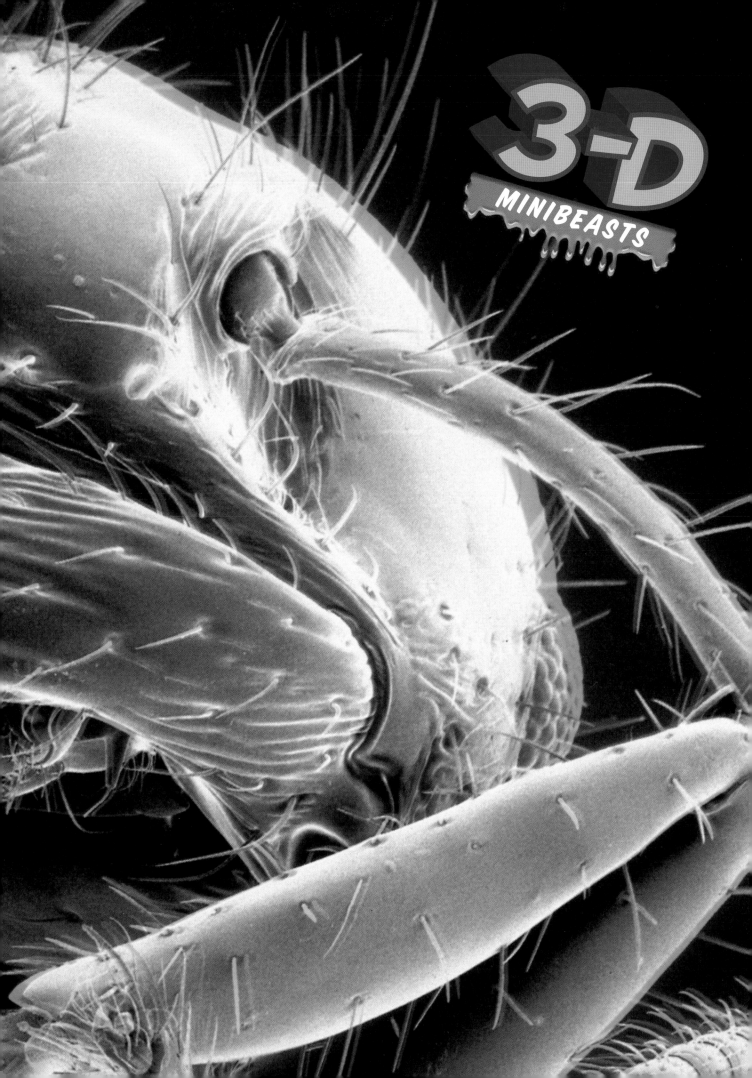

3-D
MINIBEASTS

OGRE-FACED SPIDER

Like a fisherman throwing his net to catch fish, the ogre-faced spider spreads its web over its prey.

During the day, the ogre-faced spider rests among the leaves and fallen branches of the forest. With its eight legs neatly folded underneath its body, it looks like a twig from a tree and is difficult to see. But after sunset, this large, big-eyed spider wakes up and prepares to hunt for its supper.

SETTING A TRAP

The ogre-faced spider doesn't wait patiently and quietly, like other spiders, for insects to stumble into its web. It has another plan. Each night it builds a thick sticky and stretchy web. Then, hanging upside down, it holds the web in its four front legs—and waits!

LOOK OUT BELOW

When an insect comes near, the ogre-faced spider stretches the web out wide, drops it down over its victim, and scoops it up. The spider usually eats its web when it has finished hunting at the end of each night. But sometimes it tucks it away among the twigs and branches for use the next night.

SIZING UP

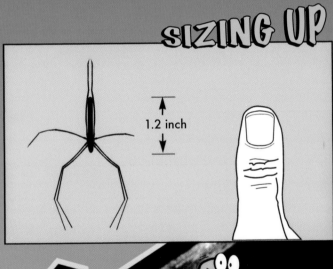

1.2 inch

BEASTLY FACTS

- **SCIENTIFIC NAME:** *Dinopis guatamalensis*
- **SIZE:** 0.47–1.2 inch
- **LIVES:** Tropical forests of Central and South America
- **EATS:** Insects

PRAYING MANTIS

The praying mantis disguises itself so it can launch a vicious surprise attack on its victims.

There are about 1,800 species of praying mantis. They live in trees and grasslands in warm places where there is a regular supply of food.

DELICATE WINGS

The praying mantis has a long, slender body and three pairs of legs. It also has two pairs of very fine wings, but in general only the smaller male uses these for flying.

PERFECT DISGUISE

With its green or brown coloring and its sticklike body, the praying mantis looks like a leaf or twig. Some of the more unusual species of praying mantis are more colorful, and look like flowers. These clever disguises help the insect blend into its background so that predators—and prey—cannot easily spot it.

PRAYING MANTIS

Small Talk

FRIEND OR FOOD?

For the male praying mantis, mating is a dangerous time. The male is slightly smaller and more delicate than the female, and when they are mating, she might mistake him for food and try to eat him! Even if the female praying mantis bites off his head, though, he can still go on mating because his body takes a while to die.

PRAYING FOR FOOD

The praying mantis has another trick that makes it even harder to see. It can stay very still, without moving at all, for hours on end. Sitting up on its hind legs with its forelegs folded neatly together in front, it looks like it's praying—which is how it got its name. Perched in this position, it waits to pounce on any unsuspecting insect that comes along.

A flexible neck helps the mantis look around and find its prey.

Large compound eyes help the praying mantis see in all directions so it doesn't miss a thing.

Spiny forelegs grip onto the victim. After each killing, the mantis cleans its spines, readying itself for the next attack.

Powerful jaws mean that the praying mantis can munch through the tough outer shells of insects.

Long, sharp claws dig into the victim.

Its front legs and body look like leaves so that the mantis can hide in trees and bushes.

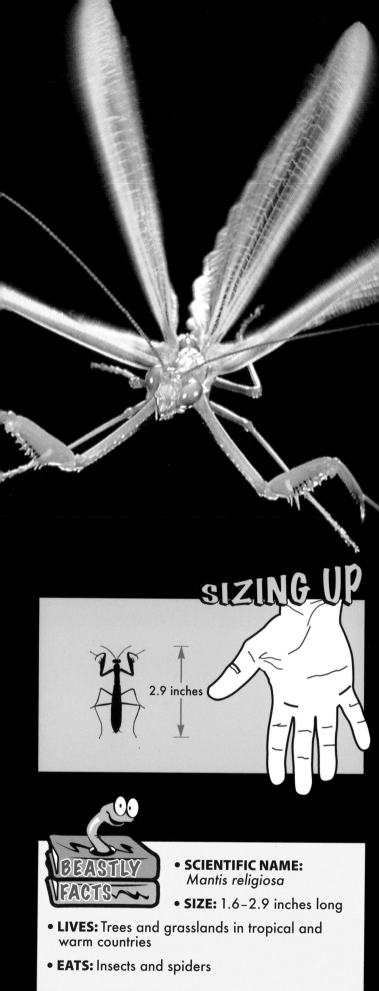

This male praying mantis is in midflight. The forelegs, usually folded in front of his body, are stretched out in front for balance.

WATCHING

The huge saucer-shaped eyes on the sides of its head along with a flexible neck allow the praying mantis to see in all directions—it can even see behind itself. It can watch its prey approaching from anywhere without turning its head. When its victim is close enough, the mantis leaps on it, gripping it firmly with its strong, spiny forelegs so that it cannot escape. Its jaws are strong enough to chew through even the toughest insect. The praying mantis is a fussy eater, though, so it may not finish its meal.

HUNGRY BABIES

Even the tiny praying mantis babies are hungry hunters. They hatch from eggs that the female lays inside a large cocoon, or hard shell. She lays about 200 to 400 eggs at a time. The tiny insects that come out of the eggs are pale green and only 0.24 inch (6mm) long, but they begin hunting almost at once—and may even eat each other.

NO DEFENSE

Although the praying mantis is a fierce hunter, it is not very good at defending itself. Its main hope is that predators—such as certain kinds of birds—won't notice that it is there. If an enemy does threaten it, it rises up to its full height, spreads out its wings, and tries to look big and scary. This doesn't always work, though, and the praying mantis just gets eaten.

SIZING UP

2.9 inches

BEASTLY FACTS

- **SCIENTIFIC NAME:** *Mantis religiosa*
- **SIZE:** 1.6–2.9 inches long
- **LIVES:** Trees and grasslands in tropical and warm countries
- **EATS:** Insects and spiders

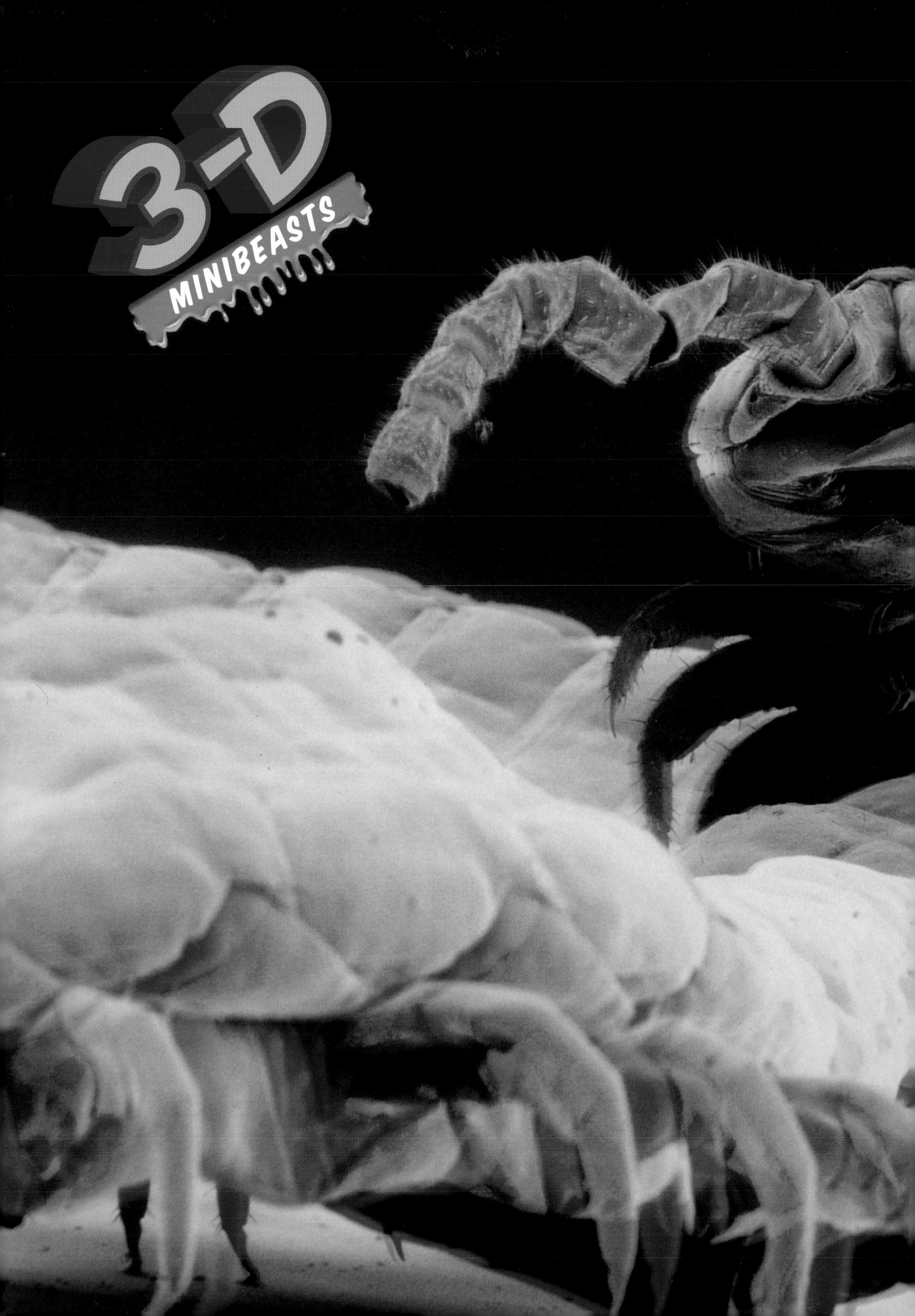
3-D
MINIBEASTS

CENTIPEDE

This is the kind of centipede you might find in your house—especially in moist places such as basements and bathrooms. It has large compound eyes as well as useful feelers. Eyes and feelers play an important role in helping the centipede find its food. Yummy treats for a centipede include silverfish, flies, cockroaches, and other small insects. Some households welcome centipedes because they keep down the numbers of these less-desirable visitors. So, come on in centipede, take the weight off your legs (all of them!), and make yourself at home.